Praise for *Blue Dog Road* ̄

Punctuated by haunting haikus & thread
memory & longing, Ann Weil's *Blue Dog Road Trip* invites
readers into the complex grief & disorientation of mothering,
mental illness & familial estrangement, the powerlessness &
surrender that is necessary even as we ask–*What is it about love /
that won't let go, even as it sinks me?* Part of living with
estrangement also means living with unanswerable questions,
& Ann poses these questions without apology, without
expectation of answers. While these poems ask readers to
brave a deep dive into love & loss, they also offer artfully
wrought reflections on what it means to grieve the living & to
endure what we think we cannot, *to dig a body-sized hole in the
yard. Climb in and lie down. / Gaze at the blue sky above. Climb out.*

Joan Kwon Glass, author of *Daughter Of Three Gone Kingdoms*
and *Night Swim*

Blue Dog Road Trip is a riveting collection of the lingering
trauma of mental health struggle and the estrangement of a
precious yet troubled son. Through free verse, haiku, sonnets
and prose poems, Ann Weil chronicles her story as a parent
faced with an impossible crisis. A heartbreaking yet necessary
collection: a vivid portrait of a poet and mother's ineffable love
amidst unyielding hardship.

Jose Hernandez Diaz, author of *Bad Mexican, Bad American*

Ann Weil's second collection is for lovers of poetry, yes. But it
is also for anyone who has yet to discover poetry's
consolations, the way words can "open wide / their fleshy
arms" to help us hold the grief of loving someone we are
powerless to save. "I understand, this game of lines / and casts,
the baited hook that catches light, / catches me as I bite again,
no match / for your allure, the pull of your reeling." It is for
anyone who has wondered how to let go. "Dig a body-sized
hole in the yard. Climb in and lie down. Gaze at the blue sky

above. Climb out." And it is for those who already know that letting go means losing a version of the self. "And now that you've gone, / I am a...stunned door hanging wide on its hinges." At the heart of Blue Dog Road Trip is "all will be well, all," an astonishing haiku that uses Julian of Norwich's famous line to redefine wellness as all of it: loss, rage, resistance, as well as brief, honeyed rest stops and narrow off-ramps to hope. "[T]he pupil / of an eye / lets in the light / of the whole world." Weil's speaker is indeed a "student of the I," a mother "cracked, wide open," yet still standing, learning to "let go the breath [I]'ve been holding since this whole thing began," finding a new, "quiet comfort / in catch and release."

Erin Redfern, author of *Spellbreaking and Other Life Skills*

Gnashing Teeth Publishing
242 East Main Street
Norman AR 71960
http://GnashingTeethPublishing.com

Printed in the United States of America

ISBN 979-8-9898345-4-9

Library of Congress Control Number 2024931572

Non-Fiction: Poetry

Gnashing Teeth Publishing First Edition

Blue Dog Road Trip

For my children—
all of them

TABLE OF CONTENTS

PROLOGUE

What to Do When Your Therapist Compliments You on Reaching Acceptance but Says "Peace" Is the True Destination

Begin by asking Google Maps for peace's precise location. When Google drops a pin in the middle of the Pacific, refrain from giving the finger.

Reconsider Google's answer and contemplate buying a 32-foot sailboat. Then remember you can't swim. Abandon the whole *Finding Nemo* scheme.

Reminisce on buying a fish tank for your boy, thinking guppies might make him happy.

Learn about "self-care." Buy a yoga mat, incense, and gong. Per your husband's request, return the gong.

Remember taking your son to see his beloved Regina Spektor in concert. Try to forget that you had to leave when his panic attack began.

Ask your friends how they achieve Nirvana. Roll your eyes when they say Spotify.

Do not cry when your mom-friends talk about their kids' college graduation parties. Remind yourself college is not for everyone.

Erase all memories of the day EMS bandaged your son's wrists and took him for his first ambulance ride.

Expand your lap-size big enough to cradle a six-foot young man.

Keep your son's psychiatrist(s) on speed dial.

Re-read *War and Peace*— but skip the war part.

Sign up for dance lessons. Crush fear under your tap shoes.

Take solace in the fact that the money you've spent on your son's treatment has put his shrink's kid though college.

Just be happy that, after everything you've been through, your son is alive. (Although— new twist— he no longer wants to see you.)

Read a book: *Done with the Crying: Help and Healing for Mothers of Estranged Adult Children.* Find perverse comfort in knowing you're not alone.

Dig a body-sized hole in the yard. Climb in and lie down. Gaze at the blue sky above. Climb out.

PART ONE

Poem as Preface

This is a book about being a mother.
About milky pearls napping in dark oyster beds.
About torn awnings letting in light, as well as rain.

This book is about mothers who open
their crisply folded cookie, read the fortune:
May you lead an interesting life.

This book is about mothering
a child with mental illness—
how in the maze of occasional sun-strewn boulevards

and briefly peaceful pathways, there are also
wrong turns, dark alleys, sometimes
no way out but past the minotaur.

This is a book for mothers in the labyrinth—
may you find your own way through.

two girls in, we seek
a boy, consult the stars,
birth our own pulsar

October, Twenty-nine Years Ago

We waited for you
in the new brick house

with the freshly sodded yard,
subdivision shiny as a new penny.

Your sisters chalked rainbows
on the sidewalk, made pinecone pies

in the sandbox. Your father mowed
and planted a tree; I fussed

over the nursery, grew large
and larger. The day you were born

was perfect– skies and eyes
as blue as ocean,
not a cloud, nor a blue dog, in sight.

roly-poly love
happy toddler, gentle soul
likes to play with cords

sisters adore him—
new sandbox pal, dress-up doll,
prince of silly sounds

born comedian,
keeps the family laughing,
especially me

Carwash as Crystal Ball

Twice in a month's time, I pulled
the minivan into the carwash,
and twice I heard your whimper,
turned to see the fear in your eyes,

your furrowed brow, your trembling body.
Twice, I twisted around in my seat
to cradle your hand in mine,
to murmur reassurance

as the monster roared and swallowed us,
his tongues and saliva lapping
at the windows, his furry paws
sweeping over the car, shoving

us further into his gullet. You cried,
and it was my fault. The first time,
my unthinking mistake. The second time,
I was sure your fear would subside.

That was just the beginning of wrong.
Some lessons take a while to learn.

places boys will pee—
front yard when company comes,
also nightstand drawer

Tell Me What to Do

He calls me to his bedside
and at first, I think maybe
he's seen another earwig
or a spider's shadow, crawling.
I arrive, prepared to be his hero.
But tonight, the walls are spare
and even the shadows have gone.
My son sits up, leans toward me
and whispers: *Mom, I don't see
myself in the future.*

We ask our kids
what they want to be when they grow up,
hoping they say doctor, engineer, scientist,
smiling when they say penguin, Santa Claus, Batman.

My child says... *nothing.*

Tell me what to do.

Blue Dog slips quiet
into our home, finds his room
lays down at his feet

Has He Seen a Therapist?

If I start in on the parade,
give a piece of my mind
to the three-ring circus, you'll never
hear its end. We never saw its end—
the snaking line of credentialed carers,
some with beating hearts that ached
in rhythm with ours, others
only interested in stretching us
like saltwater taffy— just how far
will our money take them? Sandusky?
The Jersey Shore? One told me
my son was sicker than I knew
(he was right). Another wanted
a second year of daily therapy sessions
(one year of this didn't work, so let's
double the dose). A third
barked from the boardwalk, selling
her own snakewater, whispering
Keep the money flowing—
you are lucky your son's still here.

And like the dupe in every audience,
I fell for the wanting—

a truth different
than the truth
of reality.

Now, He Does Not Eat

Such a round thing he was,
rolling curves, chubby cheeks,
tummy-first toddling like a tiny drunkard.

Me, chasing after, keeping my little pinball
from ricocheting off sharp corners
or disappearing down a bottomless chute.

I beat the machine— he made it through
early childhood unscathed.

Now, star of his own arcade game,
he's lived and died a thousand times,
fought epic wars with unfathomable monsters,

rising again and again from the gray mists,
each time picking up more wisdom points,
stronger armor. He slew The Thirst,

weakened The Darkness, escaped from the claws
of The Abuser. He's in the game. Leveling up

is a bitch but he stays with it. I'm stuck
on the sidelines watching, can't play in his game
although I have tried.

I'd stand side by side with him in battle,
but the adventure isn't played that way.
I'm pit crew, he's driver. We still need each other.

This latest level is the darkest yet.
Now, he does not eat.
Skin taut over bones. How can he fight

without fuel? Where will the life force
come from to survive the next ambush,

journey the next trek? This crew chief is in

way over her head. But I don't quit. Victory
is so close— just past the next turn of track,
the next bonus stage, the next bank shot.

I buy him New Dog
but Blue Dog refuses to leave,
clings to him like skin.

Blue Dog Road Trip

Do you remember that detour
along the unlit highway,
with no marked exits, no service plazas,
only pavement painted with worry lines?
Dotted yellow for caution, solid
for don't go off your meds no matter
the fucking side effects, and the dreaded
double crimson that means *cross me and you're dead*—
people don't often see those bastards 'til it's too late.
Remember the time you hit a pothole,
and the edge of our tires grazed the red
before you swerved back? We were so scared.
But we kept on rolling, you and me—
it's not like we had much choice, plus
we both wanted to know what might be
beyond the next bend. And there it was,
some relief at last, a *Super K* truck stop—
lights blazing, hot coffee, short stack on the griddle,
waitress calling us *Honey*. Seemed like
we could stay forever, but you were anxious
to see the sunrise at the edge of the world,
so I asked for two cups of joe to go.
Blue Dog slept curled in the back seat,
so quiet— for a while, we forgot he was there.

When You Cut Yourself

and the trickle ran from your wrist onto the white porcelain, did you think of the cardinals in the birch trees? We'd waited for that hike for weeks— finally the sun reigned over Ann Arbor and the temperature was kind for a Michigan January. You spotted the birds first, their scarlet gowns against the ivory bark, stars of the red carpet in reverse. Months before that— a snaking line of pill-pushers, traders in talk therapy, purveyors of programs, of cures in pretty packages. Each unwrapped, tried on, discarded— nothing lessened the load you carried. Then, when least expected, you'd rally, the briefest puppet show of laughing son, jesting brother. What light snuck in? I'll buy a sky's worth. I'll trade my soul. In the months when your room was your world, the wall your window, I learned to sit. We learned to wait. In the spring we planted Time— now we feast on its harvest. The geese are noisy and the air smells smoky, of burning leaves. When we walk, we see our breath.

Needlepoint

On the way to the hospital,
I plant slanted stitches
no bigger than sesame seeds
Neat, tidy, tight
rows upon rows upon rows
blanket the once-blank canvas

On the way to University
to clean out his dorm room
I stitch and breathe
with precision,
careful not to stop
not to stop
not to stop

On the way to the rehab facility
my needle points
down then through I pull
the thread
up then through I pull
the thread

until each of a thousand holes
is no more

There is life before,
and life after. The challenge
is to keep living.

Theory of Relativity

When you come so close
to a very bad *thing*—
the worst *thing* possible—
all that comes after
is compared.

That *thing* becomes
a yardstick,
a scale, a measure
encoded, embedded
deep in your cells.

It can't be shed
like sloughed skin,
remaining even after
rough scrubbing, like scent—
yours only and forever.

This ruler serves well
as you size life up
facing new strange
and frightening *things.*
You shrug them off,

not worth a fuss,
all coming up short
to what came before.
Just so many fish
too small to keep.

As if harm can be
outrun, we go to the end
of the road. Key West.

Bone Island. Refuge.
Oasis on turquoise sea.
Together, we fish.

To Check for Breath

Every mother
hears the silent call,

rises up
from deepest sleep

pads to a bedside—
checks for breath.

I am no different,
though my son is grown.

I wait and watch
for his chest to move,

to rise and fall, rise and fall,
that soothing sign that all is well

only then do I realize
I've held my own breath,

so if his had stopped,
he could have mine.

Activities for the Mother of a Son with Mental Illness

1. Cut a slit and peel back a dewy blanket of grass.

2. Crawl beneath the sod, pull it like a cover over your head.

3. Let the earth, warm with the spring sun, heal your ache.

4. Stand on the street corner and rage-scream at the traffic.

5. Fall to your knees, gutted by panic's knife.

6. Run fast and far, a rabbit fleeing the dog's snapping jaw.

7. Climb to the jagged peak of understanding.

8. Know too little and too much.

9. Cover your wounds with powder and blush.

10. Bargain with the Devil, make a deal with God.

11. Open the sarcophagus of your chest.

12. Squeeze your heart, bring it back to life.

13. Knock gently on his door, wait for the invitation.

14. Ask, *How are you today?* Prepare his favorite foods.

15. Tell him he is loved. Hold him as he weeps.

The Family Tree

so lovely from a distance,
leafy green and vibrant,
envy of a bevy of other deciduous timbers,
upon closer inspection is found decidedly diseased—
a weeping willow, a quaking aspen, a pale, peeling birch.

The mind of a tree is a terrible thing to waste.
Our old growth roots run deep through the DSM-5.
One branch anxious, one depressed. Oh look! A burl of OCD.
Yes, yes, a twisted trunk of ADHD, too.

Our sweet little seedlings don't stand a chance,
and I, too (of the panic disorder limb) wear the family's
blighted bark, bear the guilt of gamete gifting.

Does every tree
produce
such
troubled
fruit?
Or
should
we call
the
woodsman?

Landlords

In my family, we rent rooms
in our heads
to the worst of tenants.

They arrive at all hours,
enter without knocking, haul
their junk upstairs and set up house.

They make noises in the attic,
play nasty pranks,
paper the walls
with angst and obsession,
forget to flush fear,
fill the tub with tears,
flood the basement with Eau D'epression #5.
And the rent? They say they'll pay
the fifth Friday of every month.

So you see, we're over-run,
over-wrought
with these misery-loving squatters
who claim and consume
each neural hallway,
corner and cortex,
every hippocampus hiding in the closets,
all the family amygdalae
buried deep
in our heirloom armoires.

The Blame Game

Is it my fault?
asks every mother
everywhere.

Little engine
chugging up the hill—

I did my best
I did my best
I did my best

and down again—

not good enough
not good enough
not good

Forgiveness

I meant to watch the documentary on forgiveness, but I forgot to pay my cable bill. I read a book about mining instead. Did you know mining is about *the prospect of discovery and extraction of useful material*? That it's about scraping the surface in search of mettle? But apparently that kind of mining, called cracking (up) by the pros, leaves angry scars and open pits. Better to tunnel deep— says chapter three— dig down through the muck and rock, through the all-too-often lightless shafts in search of your quarry. The author warns not to fall for fool's gold distractions, urges perseverance when the way is blocked by metamorphic rubble, or by a mulish diamond wall of self-defense. I liked the part about courage, how it is sorely needed, and dynamite, too, to clear the most stubborn obstacles. TNT should do the trick, but first, I'll free the canary.

The Last Frontier

Today, my son
wore a coiled cap of magnets
on his beautiful, suffering head.

> *The electromagnet painlessly delivers*
> *a magnetic pulse that stimulates nerve cells*
> *in brain regions involved in mood control*
> *and depression.*

My understanding is a fistful of fog,
a mirror of mist that will not clear.
Like a child, I make up stories
to brush the clouds from my eyes:

> Doctor Captain steers the foundering vessel,
> charts in his log the pull of the tides,
> the reach of the moon, as if willing the forces
> to straighten the bent, right the wrong.

To ease, to ease, to ease.
This, after endless seas littered
with therapist receipts, medicine vials,
treatment program brochures, missed opportunities.

A fourteen-year odyssey.
To ease, to ease, to ease.
Hope, a schooner
sailing into the horizon.

all will be well, all
will be well, all will be well
all will be well, all

PART TWO

From Blood to Poem

After Yannis Ritsos

Wound begets leak
begets trickle
begets flow.

Claret spills upon paper.
Process never
without pain.

If you are reading this poem
I need your help.
Tell me who said

"If you want me
to write about you,
break my heart."

Once More in the Depths of Your Mental Illness

I miss you, my blue boy, vanished again
like the ripple of a skipped stone. I have
never understood your leaving— a thing
that must be borne. How long must I remain
underwater this time? Grief bubbles up
as I remember how to breathe with gills.
I swim as best I can to make the days
seem shorter, relearn deep sleep to ride out
the squalls of night. What is it about love
that won't let go, even as it sinks me?

And yet, I understand, this game of lines
and casts, the baited hook that catches light,
catches me as I bite again, no match
for your allure, the pull of your reeling.

Estrangement

The mystery not
who cut the thread,
but why. A death
without dying.
Mourning all day long.

His shadow comes
to every Sunday dinner.
We don't set a place
for him. We would,
but we have learned

shadows do not eat,
even when hungry.
In our contagion,
we, too, have lost
our appetite. We turn

sideways— disappear—
as though following him
into air once there,

and then no longer.

Break-up

I had hoped for a bone
of compromise,
would have settled
for ambiguity.
Scarcely dared
the definitive dream
of amends and reconciliation.

But here it is—
you have left us.

Back turned, Hope walks away.

run away I must—
a geographical cure
back to Bone Island

I fish alone now
finding a quiet comfort
in catch and release

After the Estrangement, I Cry

You were an October sun—
oh, so wished for, wanted.

Beautiful boy. Our last child.
Blue-eyed mystery never to be solved.

Love is a risk, at times rumpled,
shaken— perhaps, even left.

And now that you've gone,
I am a body undone.

A stunned door hanging wide on its hinges.

Dressing the Buddha

I sometimes forget he is there, sitting
zazen under the Japanese maple,
almost hidden behind the hydrangeas
heavy with white blooms— snowballs in July.

The little statue, as placid as you
were in childhood, doesn't need me in this
season of sun, but come autumn, I place
a doll-sized hat on his head, matching scarf

around his neck. Buddha snug and cherished,
as you were. Wondering where you've gone, I
remember when you knit warm gifts for all
of us, living and stone. As if you knew

the end of the story. Somehow you saw
the coming ice, impossible to thaw.

Triggered

The smell of garlic and rosemary
and roasted red meat
permeated my busy kitchen.
Kris cutting cucumbers for a green salad,
Tony spooning clouds of mashed potatoes
into a serving bowl. I checked
the starring act, found it rested and ready
for my sharp knife, my strong hand,
and as I carved the first slice
I thought of you, with the razor blade
pressed to your skin, imagined
your strong hand pushing down
to slash. I saw your blood,
as the tenderloin's red juices
spread across the cutting board.

I See Everything I Have Done

After Alecia Beymer's "I See Everything I Have Not Done"

When my head finds the pillow,
I see everything I have done today—
at my desk, a forgotten cup

of brewed-black tea. In the sink,
a delftware bowl waits to be rinsed,
bits of muesli clinging

to its blue branches, porcelain skies.
I do this all the time now—
start a task, forget to finish.

Some success: recycling bins lugged
to the curb, bills paid before Collections calls,
potions and wrinkle creams layer-caked

onto my face. Nothing works
on that front, but I can't give up trying.
Texts sent to you; texts checked ten times

to see if you'd replied. Of course,
you hadn't, but I can't give up hope.
Poems read, lines written, then wadded

and tossed, another three-point-shot
missed because the basket is full.
Laundry washed, folded, put away

for tomorrow. Amazon box retrieved
from the porch— a new book:
The Mother's Guide to Surviving Estrangement.

I used it as a coaster for another cup of tea.
Groceries bought, dinner prepped,
eaten with Wolf Blitzer in the Situation Room

where everything is broken news.
I don't need to be told
what I'm already living.
Weeds pulled as light fades
and mosquitoes whine. Notes
from therapy read and reread:

Move from acceptance to peace.
Warm shower, more potions,
phone scrolled in bed.

I say— *Alexa,*
turn out the lights.
In every dream, I see your face.

Fall Migration

Kelsi texts to say the crotons are thriving—
finally shaken-off the mystery blight— their ashen leaves
now restored to yellow-splattered glory,
a shivaree of sunshine in our backyard jungle.

I am grateful some healing needs only time,
of which these days I have plenty. Sixties are the new forties,
they say, and I feel good, better than I look.
Kelsi writes that the purple lantanas are breathtaking,

but the traveler's palm bangs angrily at the roof
on windy days. *I'll take care of it*, I tell her,
I'm coming south soon. Nothing left here to tend.
My Michigan garden sleeps under an early frost.

My son, still estranged, refuses to see me.
The harvest moon ghosts— I've nothing left to gather.

Happy Holidays.
He leaves us between first snow
and last mistletoe.

three-hundred-sixty-
-five days later his presents—
still wrapped and waiting

Being a mother

is a pear's journey. Round
and rounder in the hips,
golden or blush, spotted
by our time in the sun,
oft bitten, more often bruised,
but sweetness
underneath the skin.

And once this firm flesh
is eaten by our young,
consumed by service,
by wee-hour worry, a wiry core
rests exposed, left to cradle
seeds laid bare in the sunlight,
ready, waiting.

Unless, of course,
your child
swallows you whole.

Yes, I said "swallows
you whole." Sometimes motherhood
is like that. Trust me.

The Skin of a Mother

is not taut, like a clothesline drying diapers in the sun. It's not easy to wear, like sweatpants, not weather-proof, like the Chewbacca costume homemade for a frigid Halloween. The skin of a mother is not returnable, like that too-low-cut Homecoming dress and the four-inch heels; it's not discardable, like the red plastic cups littering a dormitory lawn. The skin of a mother is a straitjacket. No one tells you this, but it's true. After the initiation rite comes the swaddling. The whole world shrunk to one room, one woman with the power of God. At first, it's all so snug and safe— then, like a blood pressure cuff, the squeeze starts to hurt, you can't catch your breath. Your heart is a snare drum, lungs demand more air. You are desperate to run, the light flickers. Stars emerge and you long to join their brightness. But a small cry snakes its way through your ear into your brain, and you know you cannot leave. You let go the breath you've been holding since this whole thing began, giving room to your limbs, space to your spine. You wriggle and squirm like a moth shedding its cocoon. With grasping arms, you reach for that bawling life,

and begin again.

Yes, He Cut All Ties, But I'm Fine, Really I Am

If I linger at the window,
pause longer than I should
at the traffic light,
I am only noticing the blue
of today's sky.

I haven't slipped
into the momentary abyss,
missing my boy. My *young man*,
to be more accurate.
Mourning requires accuracy.

Otherwise, a brain
plays mind games—
bringing me to my knees,
demanding that I grieve
while he still breathes,

while any day now
he might call or text.
If you ask me a question,
and I don't answer,
when I stare into space

long enough to cause concern—
don't fret. It's not like I'm wallpapering
the living room with my sins,
repainting the kitchen in Regret Rose.
How silly that would be.

If I seem more shadow
than flesh and blood woman,
don't worry. I haven't moved
into a neighborhood
of the not-quite-living.

No, I'm not tethered
to my son's suffering—
searching for a cure, a magic fix,
or at least a civil reconciliation.
I'm fine. I'm simply writing in my head

one poem after another.
There is always an untried form,
a fresh metaphor, a clever rhyme,
a way to meter through
the unimaginable.

Secrets of Flight

I did not know that words
might lift themselves
from their paper perches,
stretch their serifs
into tiffany wings.

Nor did I realize I could
climb aboard their sinewy backs,
take flight from what is,
shed the chrysalis
too tight for my heart.

Alice's Cure for Everything

The book wears a red jacket, puffs
its lapels, lures me close
to stroke its spine.

Rain has made a purple morning,
clatters on the tin roof.
Armchair travel calls.

I, never an indifferent animal,
prepare reverently
for the journey:

glasses cresting
the hill of my nose,
lumbar pillow placed

between vertebrae
L1 and L5,
steaming tea mugged,

its plumed breath
wafting my way.
I am Alice in the wonder

of BookLand,
poised at the rabbit's hole—
Departure Gate page 1—

let me read, let me read.

Words open wide
their fleshy arms, I settle
into an imagined lap.

By page 10, I have left
this world behind;
by 20, my sorrows scatter

like spilled salt. By page 300,
I'm not thinking
of you at all.

Never Truly

My therapist is not an oracle,
and yet, every two or three moons,

I lay my basket of serpents at her feet.
My fears, an offering.

She peels back the dark
cloth, notes that the writhers

have diminished in size and power.
All is well, she declares,

and my left mind nods,
while my right hesitates, remembers

how quickly small problems grow large,
how they hunger for control

of one's thoughts. Oh, how I know—
we are never truly

out of the woods.
Even this now steady ground

waits patiently to bear
the fossils of our footprints.

Playing My Hand in the Murky Way

I had it all planned
this peaceful life
playing cards under the stars

never dreaming
I'd be dealing
with less than 52

but here I am
in the cosmic wreckage
mothering planets

muddling through
unruly stardust
still searching

for saner skies
for answers
and that missing jack of hearts

Missing limb. Phantom
pain ebbs and flows. At low tide,
beach is walkable.

Let me modify.
At low tide, some sunny days,
beach is glorious.

Ambassador of Her Species

The gray-haired woman knows what she knows and is unafraid to translate should anyone care to listen. She sits on her porch half-hidden by a jungle thicket—lush lady palms, leggy arecas, pale pink bougainvillea arcing skyward like a fading comet. The air is a damp rag on her skin. She drinks tea, sometimes gin, plays gin, too, right hand against the left. It has been 605 days since the jack fell from the deck, and the house still stands. A neighbor sent a card, *Keep Calm and Carry On*, and the woman lit it on fire, watched as the paper burned and spiraled upward, traces disappearing. She knows well about "not being seen." At the turning of each decade, she has reinvented herself on cue, keeping herself alive first for others, finally, for herself. The woman observes, then jots notes in her field guide, this extraordinary molting of responsible skin, a release of all that is mammalian. Curiosity gives way to understanding. She studies the lizards in her yard, the way they stare her down unblinking, the way they bask, still, under the radiant sun. Not a bad life, this last one.

Advice from My Uber Driver, Aptly Named Angelia

Hope is a fine and feathered thing,
but, Sister, you can't survive on it.
Too low-cal.
You got to fill yourself
with full-fat joy,
pour into yourself
all the homebrewed
100-proof love
you can guzzle.
And belch. Don't forget to belch.
Baby, you got to let that love
bubble right back out into the world.

Afternoon Walk, Bone Island

There were blushed mangoes
ripe on the branches
when the egg fell from the sky,

and as it hit the pavement, it cracked
wide open to the world—
a honeyed sun

pillowed among billowy clouds.
It was there I saw myself—
a blood egg, yes,

but still recognizable.

EPILOGUE

Reconciliation Affirmation: To Be Sung Daily in Front of a Mirror While Wearing a Bird Suit

There is always a way in.
A narrow crack
in the façade, a slip
of air
between window
& sill.

I once found
an opening
between
two clouds.

Another
under a stone
buried deep
in my clay heart.

Keep looking.

All you need
is a sliver—

the pupil
of an eye
lets in the light
of the whole world.

AUTHOR'S NOTE

Choosing a title, and in this case an over-arching metaphor, for one's book is a challenging task. And when the subject matter is mental illness, the choice is downright daunting. Euphemisms to describe depression date back to ancient times, and most are inadequate to describe depression's seriousness. Many are offensive and hurtful. Because of these very real issues, certain entities have suggested a veering away of metaphor to describe mental illness. While I understand this concern and agree that careful thought must accompany usage of metaphor, idiom and euphemism, I cannot, as a poet, abandon metaphor in my craft. Nor do I believe people in general should refrain from using language that helps them understand and explain their experiences. Making sense of the world may allow us to live more comfortably in that world. This is what humans do.

The origin of the term "black dog" as a euphemism for ongoing sadness or depression is contested, and I will point you to Paul Foley's excellent article* for a deeper dive. Foley cites several primary source writings of the 1700s, including at least one dictionary, that reveal the term's presence in the lexicon in the 18th century. "Black dog" became firmly rooted in modern lexicon after Winston Churchill found the metaphor useful in describing the pervasive mood of despondency that plagued him later in life.

The proverbial black dog is often described as trailing a person around or curling up in someone's lap. I appreciate the metaphor of a trailing dog in that it lends itself to both adults and children. I've had dogs all my life. Great dogs, good dogs, and one or two that at times were not so great. All these dogs were part of our family. Like it or not, mental illness, especially anxiety and depression, is also part of our family. We acknowledge its presence, seek treatment when necessary, and continue to live the best lives we can.

Using the descriptor "black" to describe depression, however, is to participate in society's ongoing association of blackness as bad or negative, which contributes to systemic racism. I felt it important to choose another color for the dog metaphor in this book, and "blue," with its longtime connotations of sadness, was the obvious choice.

As for "road trip," all of motherhood is a journey, and the one my son and I took through his years of illness was indeed a long trek, both of us in the front seat, trading off driving and surviving, with Blue Dog always nestled in the back. We liked him best when he was sleeping.

*@inproceedings{Foley2005BlackDA,
title={'Black dog' as a metaphor for depression: a brief history},
author={Paul Bernard Foley},
year={2005},
url={https://api.semanticscholar.org/CorpusID:148178042}
}

ACKNOWLEDGEMENTS

Some of the poems in this book have been previously published elsewhere. I am incredibly grateful to these journals and their editorial staff.

The Dunes Review	"The Last Frontier"
FOLIO	"Secrets of Flight"
The Healing Muse	"Activities for the Mother of a Son with Mental Illness" (published as "Choices for the Mother of a Son with Mental Illness")
The MacGuffin	"Ambassador of Her Species"
Mockingheart Review	"Needlepoint" (published as "The Point") and "When You Cut Yourself"
New World Writing	"Afternoon Walk on Bone Island" and "Break-up"
The Shore	"Estrangement"
South Florida Poetry Review	"Alice's Cure for Everything"
Sweet: A Literary Confection	"Once More in the Depths of Your Mental Illness"
Thimble Literary Magazine	"Never Truly"
West Trade Review	"The Skin of a Mother"

It takes a village to raise a poet. First, I extend my most heartfelt gratitude to the extraordinary teachers with whom I've studied these past few years— thank you to Joan Kwon Glass, Jose Hernandez Diaz, and Erin Redfern for your thoughtful instruction and generosity of spirit. A special thank you goes to Joan Kwon Glass for her skillful editing of this manuscript. You inspire me every day, Joan. Sincere thanks and big love to my writing groups, Hot Mess (Morgan Ray, Kathleen Goldblatt, Dorinda Woodley, Lynda Madison, and Laura Garfinkel—I am deeply indebted to you for your continuous support) and to the wonderful Red Ferns (especially Christine Penney, my partner in epistolary play). And to my dear writing buddies Jackie Craven, Susan Kress, Sally Ziph, and Bonnie Morrissey, I am truly grateful for your suggestions and edits— you lift my work to new heights. To Karen Cline-Tardiff and Jennifer Taylor at Gnashing Teeth Publishing, thank you for believing in my book and for your support in bringing it to print.

I am a firm believer in the benefits of therapy, and my therapist, Janet Fry, has saved my sanity time and again. Thank you, Janet. Likewise, I owe much to my fellow Al Anon attendees, whose shared experiences, strength and hope help keep me happy and healthy. Finally, my beloved family— you are my earth and sky. Thank you Tony, Jill, Kelsey, Melanie, Daniel, Brandon, Russ, Greg, Krista, Jane, John, Sandy, Archie, Scout, and Leila for your steadfast light and love. And to my son, should you ever read this, please know that I love you. I will always love you. The door is forever open.

ABOUT THE AUTHOR

Ann Weil is the author of *Lifecycle of a Beautiful Woman* (Yellow Arrow Publishing, 2023). Her poetry has received multiple nominations for the Pushcart Prize and Best of the Net and appears in *Best New Poets 2024, Pedestal Magazine, Crab Creek Review, The Shore, Chestnut Review, RHINO, DMQ Review, Maudlin House, 3Elements Review, Anti-Heroin Chic,* and elsewhere. A former K-12 special education teacher and university professor, Ann lives with her husband and soul-dog in Ann Arbor, MI, and Key West, FL.

Milton Keynes UK
Ingram Content Group UK Ltd.
UKHW050823270924
1874UKWH00001B/1

9 798989 834549